A SOURCEBOOK OF

SONNY TERRY LICKS

FOR BLUES HARMONICA

By Tom Ball

Special thanks to:
Laurie Linn Ball, Flying Fish Records, Brian Smith, Pat Missin, Mary Katherine Aldin, Kenny Sultan, Folk Mote Music, Mercer Management, Tony Russell, Galen Gart, Old Bushmills Distillery, Shannon Leigh Ward, and the family.

ISBN 978-1-57424-018-4
SAN 683-8022

Music Notation - Dave Celentano
Layout and Production - Ron Middlebrook
Cover photo, Sonny Terry (old promotional photo, c.1938.)
Back Cover of Tom Ball by Jeff Brouws
CD Engineer: Sean McCue,
All 78 labels and LP covers from the author's collection.

- <u>CONTENTS</u> -

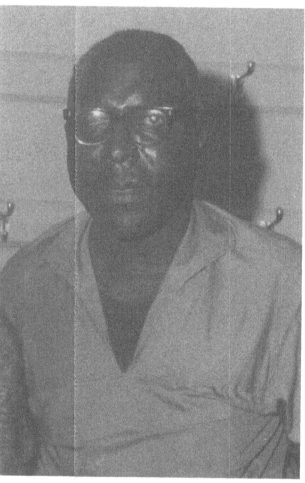

Photo by Brian Smith

> *"Sonny Terry has got to be explained to the people or his art will go over their head. And in understanding Sonny Terry, you will learn how to enjoy and live in the real people's music that is on a train that's bound for glory."* -Woody Guthrie, 1946

l. to r. Brownie McGhee, Woody Guthrie, Jackie Gibson, "Zacky", Sonny Terry, Bob Harris

About the author

Tom Ball was born on Sonny Terry's brithday. Tom is half of the popular good-time blues duo Tom Ball and Kenny Sultan. Tom and Kenny have a total of six instructional books and seven albums, the most recent of which, "Filthy Rich," is available on Flying Fish.

For information, write:

Tom Ball, Box 20156, Santa Barbara, CA 93120 USA

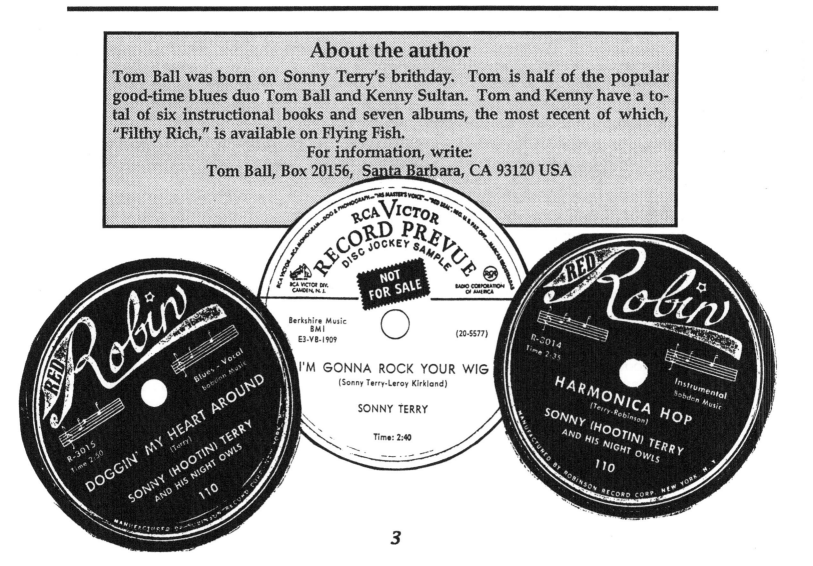

- INTRODUCTION -

A couple of years ago I had the pleasure of putting together a harmonica instructional book and cassette pack entitled **Blues Harmonica - A Comprehensive Crash Course and Overview** for Centerstream Publications. The response to that book far exceeded my expectations: letters filtered in from all corners of the globe discussing, analyzing and in some cases constructively criticizing the project.

Although the prevailing tone of the response has been positive, some harmonica players were less than satisfied with the relative lack of specific licks to play. This was by design. With the previous book, the ideas was to present as comprehensive and broad an overview as possible without overly delving into note-for-note transcriptions. This project, on the other hand, is far more specific. Here the intent is to explore, appreciate and hopefully learn from the acknowledged master of the country blues harp: the late, great Sonny Terry.

What you now hold in your hands is a **Lick Book** - nothing more, nothing less. For those of you wishing to learn more about Sonny's life, let me heartily recommend Kent Cooper and Fred Palmer's **The Harp Styles Of Sonny Terry** (Oak Publications,) which contains not only an explanation of Sonny's style, but also an often hilarious oral autobiography.

The purpose of this project is simply to supply players with transcriptions (and a CD) of licks from Sonny's repertoire. Think of it as source material. Each lick is both played on the CD and mapped out in easy-to-read harmonica tablature. Naturally it would've been ideal to have Sonny's own playing on the CD, but licensing nightmares precluded that obvious approach, so the licks are played by me.

At the risk of sounding hypocritical, it is important to remember that no musician ever truly makes a statement by copying anyone else note-for-note. Eventually, all players need to develop styles of their own, but in so doing we also all must initially learn from others. It is difficult to become a master without first digesting the masters, but it is hoped that players will learn from and then vary upon these licks. Improvisation is the nature of the beast, and the bottom line is to have fun.

Please also note that this is not a method book per se. Although there are ten pages of remedial harp lessons provided, and a look at Sonny's style, it is assumed that the reader is already somewhat accomplished on the instrument. If, for example, you do not already know how to play single notes at will, or cannot bend notes fluently, this book may be a bit advanced.... in that case, I might recommend either my aforementioned **Blues Harmonica** or one of the other fine beginners books on the market.

Above all, please go out and buy some Sonny Terry CDs. Even if you do learn some of these individual licks, it does little good if you don't know where to put 'em. And another thing: carry your harp with you wherever you go. It's small and portable, and you never know when some well-played blues might result in a free beer! As Sonny has said: "The blues seemed to give me more room for my moods. If I felt good, there was a way of fitting that in. Or, if I was more low, I could get it off me by playing it away. Music was something you could take with you, you know, without no bother."

Tom Ball

Sonny Terry, the undisputed king of the country blues harmonica, had a number of careers in music: local street musician, blues recording artist, dramatic and concert artist, R&B session man, film extra, and folk musician. Throughout it all, he maintained his instantly recognizable rural harp style; to this day, no one sounds like Sonny.

Born into a Georgia sharecropping family in 1911, he was christened Saunders Terrell (or Saunders Teddell, or Sanders Terrell, or Sanders Teddell, depending on whose "research" you care to believe.) He began to play harp at the age of 8, sneaking his father's instrument from it's hiding place and blowing away in secret. Two separate childhood accidents robbed him of his sight, and soon thereafter it became evident to both he and his family that if he were to make a go of it in the world, the harmonica might be his only way. After his blindness, "I wouldn't go out of the house because I was ashamed," Sonny said. " The only thing I had any interest in was playing my harmonica, and I kept on it night and day... it was a friend who didn't give a damn if I could see or not".

Although Terry never specifically mentioned him as an influence, almost certainly he must have been exposed to the playing of Henry Whitter, a white Virginia textile worker who recorded several 78s for the Okeh label in the mid 1920's. A few of Whitter's pieces show up in Sonny's early repertoire, including 'Lost John,' 'Fox Chase,' 'Shortnin' Bread' and 'Lost Train Blues,' a solo which Terry later recorded nearly note-for-note as 'Train Whistle Blues' for an obscure release in Columbia's classical series in 1938.

When asked, Sonny usually credited DeFord Bailey as his major source of inspiration. A gifted player and the only black member of the Grand Ol' Opry, Bailey also played in a distinctively rural style, concentrating both on first-position and on cross-harp. Among Bailey's early recordings are yet other versions of 'Lost John' and 'Fox Chase,' which, coincidentally were the first two titles released under the name of Sanders Terry by the Library of Congress in 1938. "He was good!" said Terry of Bailey, "I learned Alcoholic Blues from him, and some other licks."

By the mid-'30's Terry was also good, winning local harmonica contests and working with medicine shows. His main income, however, came from playing the streets, and as a young man he took off for North Carolina. He soon found out that the most lucrative locations for playing were in front of the tobacco warehouses, where men congregated before and after work. It was in front of one of these warehouses - in Wadesboro - that he met the great blues guitarist Blind Boy Fuller.

Terry recollected in **The Harp Styles of Sonny Terry:** "One Saturday afternoon I was blowin' my harp on a street in Wadesboro when I heard somebody playin' a guitar nearby. I said to myself, 'Damn, he sounds pretty good.'

"I sent a boy around to tell him to come over and play some with me. So about the time my boy got to him, he had done sent somebody around to tell me to join him. So I did, and that's the first time I met Blind Boy Fuller."

In a 1973 **Living Blues** interview with Barry Elmes, Sonny was more expansive: "He told me, said 'Come to Durham.' Said we may get to make a record together. I'd heard his records, y'know... stayed with him about a year."

Fuller proved to be true to his word, and Terry's first chance to record came in December of '37. After that, he appeared on at least some titles at every subsequent Fuller session, and even moved in with Fuller and his wife.

"Fuller was a pretty good nice guy, " Sonny told Kent Cooper. "He'd get evil some time but he was all right to me." Their partnership might have lasted for decades, but it ended prematurely in '41 when Fuller died of kidney failure.

A couple of years earlier, Sonny had briefly met guitarist Brownie McGhee, and up-and-coming musician from Tennessee. "It was in Burlington, North Carolina," Sonny later recalled. "Fuller and I had gone there on a Saturday to play outside the mills... A fellow that owned a stand was letting Brownie sleep in empty taxi cars. When Brownie come, he had a harmonica player with him called Jordan Webb... I myself thought Brownie played pretty good for just starting out. He was only about 20 years old then, (but) he learned pretty fast. The next time I heard him he sounded real good."

Before long, McGhee and Terry had moved to New York and were recording together, sometimes billed as 'Blind Boy Fuller No.2,' a practice which plainly disgusted McGhee. "Brownie didn't like that, no ways," Terry said. Their circle of friends also included Leadbelly, Woody Guthrie, Pete Seeger, Cisco Houston and Josh White.

Although today's music fan immediately associates Sonny Terry with Brownie McGhee, throughout the '40s and early '50s they worked separately almost as often as they did together. McGhee, for example, recorded 44 pre-war sides; only 8 featured Terry, while 24 had Jordan Webb on harp. In the years 1944-1954, roughly half of McGhee's recordings had no harmonica at all, and were often of the jump/swing blues variety, featuring saxes, piano, bass and drums.

At the same time, Terry's early sessions were often devoid of guitar: of his 26 pre-war titles, only 2 had guitar, the balance being either solos or harmonica and washboard duets.

Still, by the mid-'50s their names were inexorably linked; due to an amazingly prolific recording schedule, the public began to demand them as a duo. For the next 30+ years they played together, touring the world and performing thousands of concerts. Although their personal relationship became frayed, before he died in '86 Sonny is quoted thusly (again, to Kent Cooper:) " I don't hate nobody, I can say that. And I have to say most people been real nice to me except for one guy down in Greensboro years ago who stuck his hand in my hat and stole out a dollar. I hope the fool's still spending it."

Juke Box Tabs, 1953

REMEDIAL BLUES HARP- SOME *QUICKIE* LESSONS

As stated in the introduction, it is assumed that the player reading this already has a working knowledge of blues harp. If you are familiar with the concept of twelve-bar blues, can hit single notes at will and can bend (and unbend) notes fluently, then congratulations! You get to skip over the next ten pages or so, and help yourself to a sandwich.

What follows is a condensed version of a much longer explanation from my earlier book Blues Harmonica.

HOW TO HOLD YOUR HARP

Basically, no set way - what ever's most comfortable for you. Make sure the harmonica is face-up, though, meaning the low notes are on the left. (The little numbers are then visable on the top of the harp.)

How the harp fits into your hands will depend upon how large your hands are. Big beefy paws (like mine) are an advantage. As a general rule, the harp is supported by the left hand, leaving the right hand to pivot, cup, wah-wah and otherwise effect the sound of the thing. (Some lefties might feel more comfortable reversing this.)

A few harpists (including Sonny Terry) play the harp upside-down - i.e. low notes to the right. Obviously in Sonny's case this was no handicap. In <u>The Harp Styles of Sonny Terry</u>, Sonny told Fred Palmer, "They tell me that's wrong, you know. If it is, I don't wanna be right. See, if I hold the bass on the left, and then I start to move on the harp, well, then I ain't got nothin' left down there!" Still, Sonny was the exception rather than the rule.

Below you'll find some photos of various hand placements. Try them all and see what feels most comfortable. My own position most closely resembles the bottom right photo.

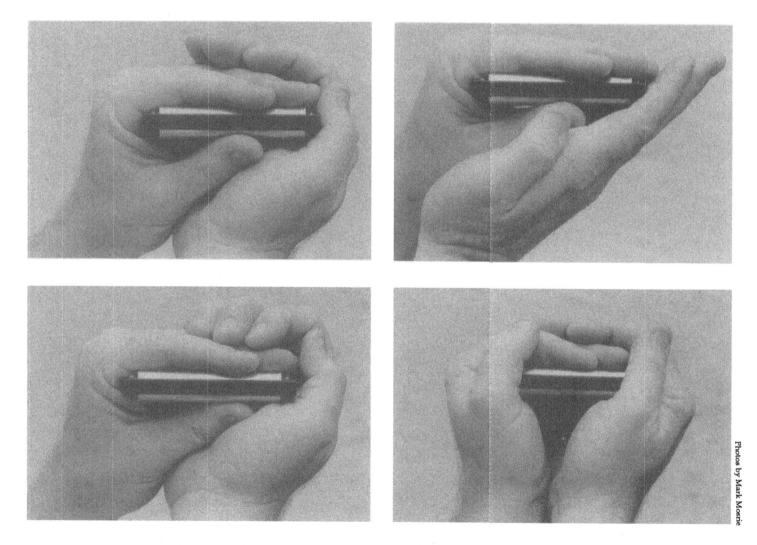

Photos by Mark Mossie

In any case, the object is to form a cup with your hands around the back side of the harp. Experiment with this until this cup is as airtight as possible. The object is not to choke off the sound, but to be able to control it by opening up the cup at strategic times without dropping your harp. The resultant effects will be covered in a few pages.

Harmonica tab really couldn't get much more basic. As you can see by looking at your harp, all the holes have numbers - 1 through 10. In the tab system, those numbers work in conjunction with arrows. An arrow pointing up designates a "blow;" a down arrow is a "draw." Thus, in the example below the player is to blow hole 4, then draw hole 4:

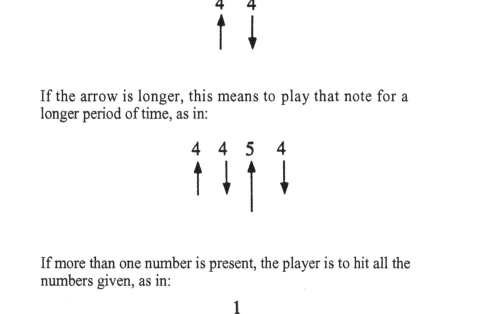

If the arrow is longer, this means to play that note for a longer period of time, as in:

If more than one number is present, the player is to hit all the numbers given, as in:

Obviously harmonica tab is not a complete notation system, but more of a shorthand. The only consideration given as to time is the arrow length, and even that is subject to interpretation. But it's the nature of the harmonica to be freely interpreted, improvised and messed with. If there is any instrument for which standard notation would be too restraining and constricting, it is the harmonica.

SINGLE NOTES

The most important first lesson on the harp is to learn to hit single notes accurately and at will. And it'll take some practice.

The initial tendency is to blow on 2 or 3 holes at the same time. To do so makes a nice chord, and sounds fine - but the essence of blues harp is single notes and bent notes. I cannot overemphasize the importance of accurate single notes.

To start out with, take your 2 index fingers and cover up every hole except 4, then blow into hole 4. That's a single note.

Now take your index fingers away and see if you can repeat this. Chances are your breath is now also leaking into one of the holes <u>next</u> to 4. Without realizing it, you may be hitting 3 and 4 (or 4 and 5.)

Be aware of the shape of your mouth. The opening of your lips must be small - think of yourself as drinking through a straw. Pucker your lips, as though you're saying "oooo," and if you're still having a problem try to alter the shape of the pucker. See if you can make the opening smaller, like a sideways oval.

Some instruction books tout another way to hit single notes: the tongue block method. With tongue blocking, the opening of the lips is larger, encompassing enough space to blow into 4 holes. Then the tongue "blocks out" 3 of them by actually touching the face of the harp, leaving only 1 hole open.

I neither use nor recommend the tongue block method and tend to think of it as a holdover from earlier styles. It is true that by adding and removing the tongue block you can get some unusual rhythm effects which are impossible otherwise - that is, if you want to go around sounding like the calliope at the carousel. Still, each to his own devices. It's just that if the tongue is tied up actually touching the harp everytime you want a single note, then it won't be free to be in the back of your mouth for some other techniques which we'll cover soon.

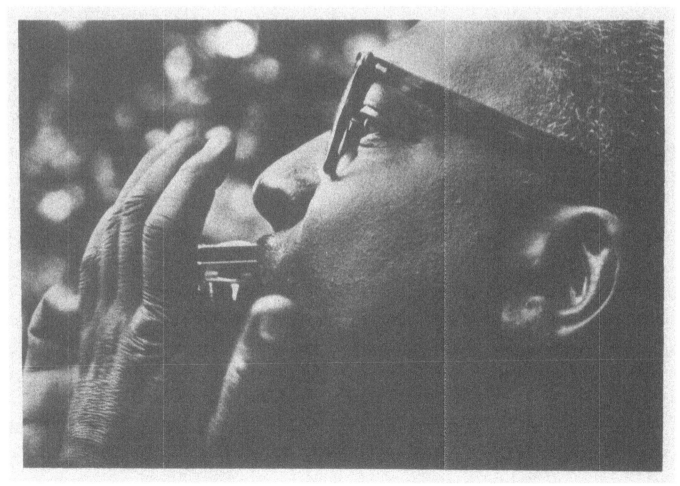

Photo by David Gahr, Courtesy of Mary Katherine Aldin

STRAIGHT HARP

Playing "straight harp" simply means playing the harmonica in the key for which it was designed - i.e. playing a "C" harmonica in "C." In order to understand the principle, we need to take a look at the way harmonicas are tuned.

All diatonic harps have 10 holes, each of which contain 2 reeds - 1 blow reed and 1 draw reed. The blow reeds are located on the top of the harp, the draw reeds on the bottom. Here's a C harp layout:

DIATONIC C HARP

	1	2	3	4	5	6	7	8	9	10
BLOW	C	E	G	C	E	G	C	E	G	C
DRAW	D	G	B	D	F	A	B	D	F	A

This configuration is known as Richter tuning, named after the Bohemian instrument maker who developed it. Notice the blow notes; they are all either C, E or G. Those of you who have studied a bit of music will recognize that C, E and G make up the 3 notes of the C-chord triad (i.e. the tonic, third and fifth of the C-scale.)

This arrangement is far from accidental. The original premise, no doubt, was to arrange the notes so that no matter where one blows multiple notes on a C harp, a C-chord (in one inversion or another) is the result.

Take a blow on holes 1, 2 and 3 simultaneously. What you're playing is a classic C-chord. Move on up the harp and blow on 4, 5 and 6, and you get the same C-chord one octave higher. Ditto 7, 8 and 9.

Now let's explore the draw notes. They're a little more varied,, and contain G, A, B, D and F. What is the relationship? These notes form a dominant ninth chord (G9) in relation to the root(C.)

Because the harp is set up this way, "straight harp" is particularly suitable for simple melodies, folk songs, campfire ditties, etc. Both the basic melodies and the appropriate chords are readily available. Whenever you hear some cowpoke play "Red River Valley" or "Oh Susanna" in a John Wayne movie, he's playing straight harp.

Is it appropriate for blues? Sure, sometimes - but not all that often. We go into the why and wheres of that in our discussion of "cross harp." But still, <u>straight harp is the place to start</u>! Ya gotta learn to walk before you can run. Straight harp is the easiest way to get familiar with the instrument, and to learn to get around on it. And everything you learn from playing straight harp will come handy later on.

A little earlier we talked about single notes, and the importance of learning to hit just one note at a time. Keep that in mind as you play the following:

$$4\uparrow \quad 4\downarrow \quad 5\uparrow \quad 5\downarrow \quad 6\uparrow \quad 6\downarrow \quad 7\downarrow \quad 7\uparrow$$

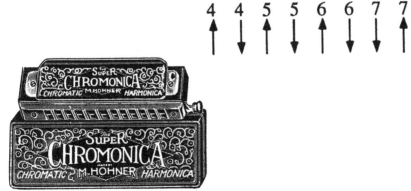

This, of course is the C-major scale (do, re, mi, etc.)
Practice this over and over again. Now try it backwards:

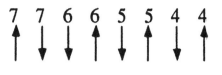

If it sounds too full, you're probably hitting more than one note at a time. Make the opening in your mouth smaller and try it again. No tongue blocking allowed!

If something sounds rattly, don't immediately assume you have a defective harp. More likely, you're simply drawing harder than you need to. Try playing it softer.

Sure, I know it's kinda stupid just to play the scale over and over again - but the purpose is to get you used to playing single notes. Once you feel like you've got it, then go on to one of these insipid little tunes:

Here's one everybody knows. It only involves blow notes.

TAPS

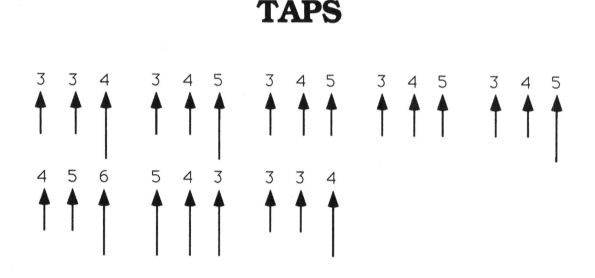

Remember that the longer arrow means to hold that note longer

Taps is very forgiving, in that if you're having problems hitting single notes it still sounds pretty much OK. This is due to the way the harp is tuned. But, again, the object here is to hit single notes.

Now let's incorporate the draw reeds. I'm assuming you all know how this one's supposed to go:

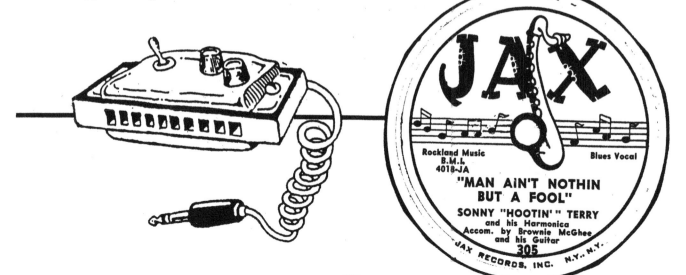

ROW, ROW, ROW YOUR BOAT

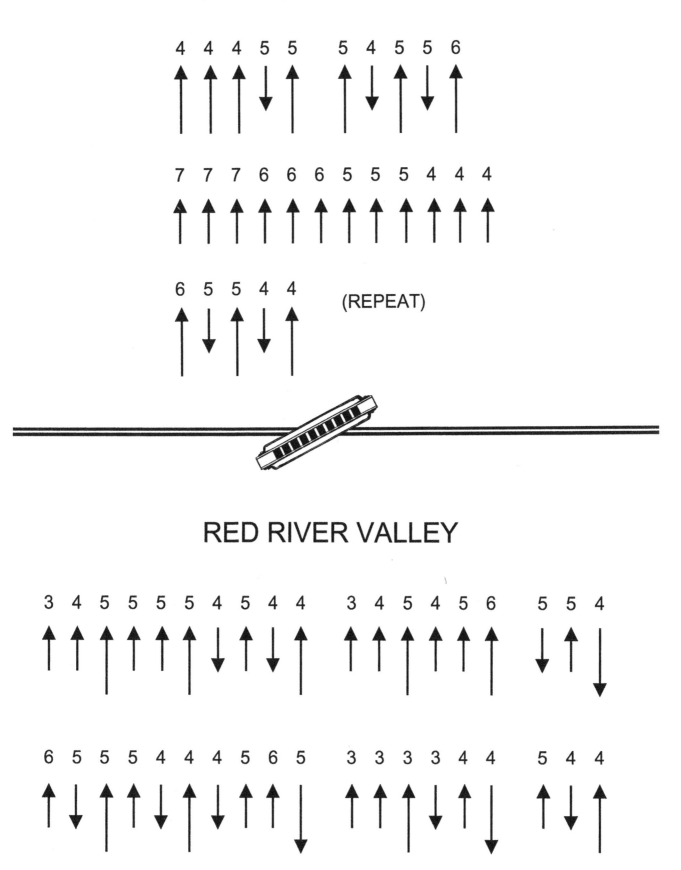

RED RIVER VALLEY

CAMPTOWN RACES

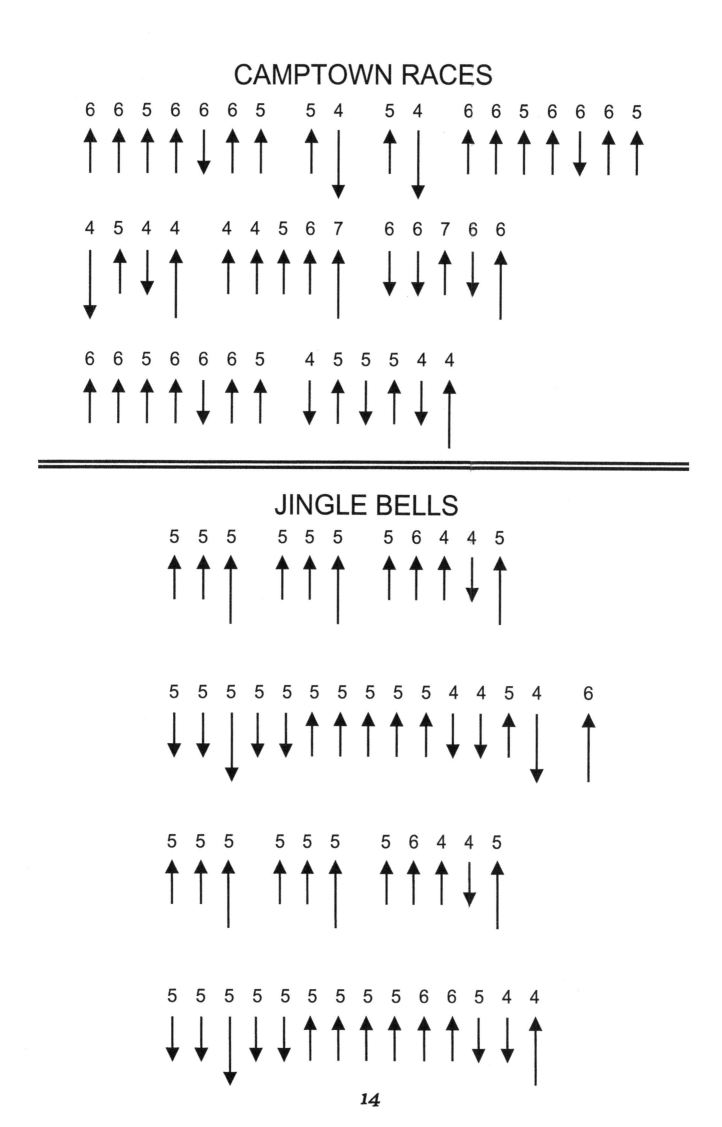

JINGLE BELLS

CROSS HARP

To understand cross harp is to understand blues harp - it's that basic. The overwhelming majority of all recorded blues harmonica (as well as bluegrass, country and rock n' roll) is played in this position and manner. So what is cross harp?

Cross harp is simply the common name for second position or Mixolydian mode - but don't let that scare you. In essence, all it means is that instead of #4 blow being the root note (as in straight harp,) now #2 draw is the root note.

Somewhere along the line, somebody discovered that if a player were to emphasize the <u>draw</u> notes and <u>bend</u> the draw notes, that a very bluesy sound was the result. And that if the root note was the #2 draw, the ensuing scale would lend itself toward that kind of sound. Hence, cross harp.

So what does it mean to the player? It means that <u>you are no longer playing the harp in the key for which it was designed</u>. In fact, the harp you use is 4 steps up the scale from the key you want to play in; thus, to play in C you'd need an F harp. Take a look at the following chart:

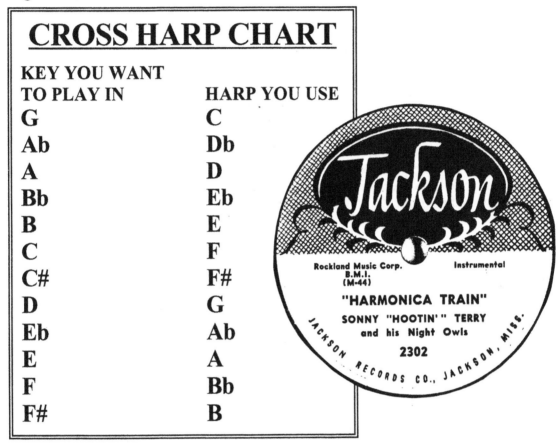

CROSS HARP CHART

KEY YOU WANT TO PLAY IN	HARP YOU USE
G	C
Ab	Db
A	D
Bb	Eb
B	E
C	F
C#	F#
D	G
Eb	Ab
E	A
F	Bb
F#	B

Let's suppose some guitar player says to you: "Hey, let's play in A." Taking a peek at this chart will tip you off that you'll need to grab your D harp.

I often recommend to beginning students that they Xerox this chart and keep it with their harps until they've memorized it. Another idea is to mark each harp case with a magic marker, noting which cross key each plays in. Eventually, though, you'll need to memorize this information.

By playing in cross position, the emphasis of the wind direction will change. In other words, <u>instead of primarily blowing your harp, you will be primarily drawing.</u> Blues harp is at least 80% draw notes, so warm up your chops and get ready to suck!

BENDING

WHAT?

"Bending" notes is simply another way to describe the flattening or downward alter-ing of the pitch of a given note. <u>Learning to accurately bend notes is the key to playing blues harmonica.</u>

HOW?

The bend is achieved by altering both the shape of the mouth and the nature of the wind supply. A tone on the harmonica can only be bent <u>downward</u> in pitch; it's impossible to bend a note upward (although it is possible to create the illusion of an upward bend - we'll explore that in a couple of pages.)

WHY?

There are several reasons for bending notes. As we discussed earlier, the diatonic harp is only capable of producing a limited number of tones, and does not include all the notes of the chromatic scale. By learning to bend the existing notes, a player expands the capability of the instrument dramatically. Perhaps even more important, the very nature of the bent note is the essence of blues. If we listen to an expert blues guitarist, for example, we'll constantly hear bent strings - the creation and release of tension employed by this glis-sando effect is a cornerstone of blues.

The basis for bent (or "blue") notes probably comes from the West African vocal scale, which employs minor thirds, flatted fifths and minor sevenths. These effects have be-come so much a part of contemporary music that they are often taken for granted by both vocalists and instrumentalists.

CROSS HARP

The main reason that cross harp is the favored position for blues has to do with the bent note. As we shall see, <u>on the lower 6 holes of the harp it is impossible to bend the blow reeds - only the draw reeds can be bent.</u> And since bent notes are the keystone of the blues sound, we will want to employ them often; thus, we must draw often. The result be-comes cross harp. (See chapter on cross harp if confused.)

GETTING STARTED - DRAW BENDS

First of all it's extremely difficult to bend 2 notes at the same time - therefore, if you're still having trouble hitting one note at a time you will not have success bending. Practice is essential... don't jump the gun. Be sure you are comfortable with single notes.

Take an inhale on hole #1. Listen to the note and memorize how it sounds. Now, as you're drawing in air, experiment with changing the pressure and shape of your mouth. Try sucking harder and moving your jaw around slightly. Various people have success with various techniques, so you might try some of the following:

1. Say "oooh - aaah - oooh - aaah" to yourself
   while drawing the note.
2. Say "oooy - oooy - oooy."
3. Raise and/or lower your jaw a bit.
4. Shift your tongue back in your mouth.
5. Pinch the wind supply by tightening the tension
   in the throat.
6. Tense your lips slightly.
7. <u>Suck harder!</u>

At least one of these techniques (or perhaps all of them in conjunction) ought to work for you. The result should be that the note dips <u>downward</u> in pitch.

Is it working? If not, keep messing with it - it'll come. Bending can be elusive at first... I recall having a terrible time with it until suddenly it just hit me. Norton Buffalo describes the phenomenon as akin to trying to suck a really thick milk shake through a straw... a big chunk of ice cream'll get stuck, necessitating more pressure, but then it eventually comes free with a thunk. That "thunk" is the bend.

Once you've gotten to the point where you can make #1 draw go down in pitch, move up the harp to #2 draw and try it there. This'll be a little harder because there are now holes both to the left and the right of the hole you're working. Again, make sure you're <u>only</u> hitting #2 draw. Give it a shot. Now try #3 draw, and #4, etc., right on up the harp.

What you'll notice is that once you get way up the harp (#7-#10) it'll get impossible to bend the draw notes. This is due to the harp's construction, not your playing, so don't worry about it.

BENDABILITY

The various holes have differing amounts of "bendability" - that is to say you can bend certain holes further in pitch than others. Hole #2 can be bent 2 semitones, hole #3 can be bent 3 semitones, and holes #1, 4, 5 and 6 can only be bent 1 + semitone. These factors apply no matter what key harp you use, and are the direct result of the Richter tuning.

Bending these draw notes (#1 - #6) is something you will want to practice again and again and again! <u>This is the single most important technique in blues harp!</u>

"UPWARD" BENDS

Again, it is not possible to bend a note upward in pitch; we can only flatten a note downward. But let's look a little closer:

Try bending hole #2 draw. Start out by drawing normally, then slowly bend it down in pitch, and then slowly release the bend until it returns to it's normal pitch. On a graph, such a tone would look like this:

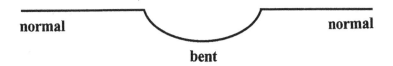

normal normal

bent

As you've just discovered, if you allow your mouth to return to "normal" while bending a note, the pitch rises back up to "normal." Let's look at that graph again:

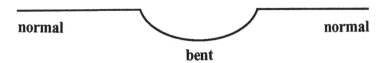

normal normal

bent

If we chop off the first part of the graph, in other words if we start the note <u>already bent</u> and simply release the bend, then the graph looks like this:

normal

bent

In a nutshell: while we can't truly bend a given note upward, we can create the illusion of an upward bend by pre-bending the note downward, and then simply releasing the bend. Like everything else, this takes practice. You'll need to attack the note in a more aggressive fashion and really bite into it.

The more comfortable you get with pre-bending, the easier everything else becomes. Another technique is to chop off both the first part and the last part of this graph... in other words, to hit only the bent part of the note. To do this adds a (previously unattainable) note to your harp. Extrapolate this over the entire harp and you've now added a lot of new notes.

HIGH-NOTE BLOW-BENDS

These are not as essential to master as the draw bends, but they do add a lot in terms of variety and dynamics.

As we discovered earlier, on the bottom holes of the harp, only the draw notes can be bent. It is a quirk in design, though, that on the top holes, only the blow notes can be bent.

The technique used to get these high-note blow-bends is somewhat different, and a bit more difficult. Right off the bat you'll notice that they are much easier to accomplish on lower-keyed harps, so try this out on a G. A, or Bb harp. (You'll find it nearly impossible on, for example, an F harp.)

First let's isolate #9 blow on an A harp. Play it lightly and listen to the tone. Now, purse your lips, blow harder, and raise your tongue upward as you blow. Hopefully, the result will be a downward lowering of the pitch. Again, this technique is not easy at first - you may have to mess around with it for awhile before it clicks. Keep trying though, and eventually it'll come to you. Incidentally if you're a feline fancier, this'll drive your cats right out of the house... also, this turns some dogs into psychopathic howling banshees, which may open up a whole career for you on Letterman's "Stupid Pet Tricks." Just put my 15% in the mail. These blow-bends are particularly handy on holes #8-#10. Take a listen to Jimmy Reed for a lesson from a master of this technique

> ## IN SUM
> Basically, blues harmonica is nothing more than a series of bent, unbent and partially bent notes strung together in cohesive phrases over a skeletal structure. Later on I'll map out (in tablature) many of the most recurrent phrases, together with a bunch of riffs and tricks - but before we go on, <u>practice bending until your lips bleed!</u>

GROOVE

A PRODUCT OF RADIO CORPORATION OF AMERICA
MADE IN U.S.A.

DISC JOCKEY — NOT FOR SALE

Hesch Music
BMI
E4-HB-3500

(G-0015)

LOST JAWBONE

(Sonny Terry)

SONNY TERRY

Time: 2:21

Sonny's first
partner,
Blind Boy Fuller

FULL
RANGE
RECORDING

PERFECT

(22160)

Blues Singing
with Guitar Acc.

HUNGRY CALF BLUES

BLIND BOY FULLER

8-04-62

SONNY'S STYLE

First things first: make sure you've got the right kind of harp! Like most blues players, Sonny Terry played a 10-hole diatonic harp (in his case a Hohner Marine Band.) Some folks prefer other similar models like the Blues Harp, Special 20, Golden Melody, Lee Oskar, Huang, Meisterklasse, etc., any of which are fine as long as they have 10 holes and no slide button.

While Sonny played his harp upside-down (low notes to the right,) it is not necessary (nor recommended) that you do the same. On the other hand (no pun intended,) if you've somehow managed to already learn to play upside-down like Sonny, it's also not necessary for you to now unlearn everything you know and switch over. It really doesn't matter.

Also, Sonny played in an acoustic manner. That is, he didn't hold a bullet mike in his hands and blow through an amp, a la Chicago blues players like Little Walter, Junior Wells, Walter Horton and others. He simply played as though there was no microphone around. This fact, perhaps more than any other, explains how he was able to achieve so many hand effects like slapping, fanning, wah-wahs, etc... he didn't have to worry about dropping a hand-held mike.

Although there are a few recorded examples of Terry playing in first position (straight harp,) the overwhelming majority of the time he played cross harp (second position.) And since I cannot recall him ever playing in third, fourth or fifth positions, for the purposes of this book those positions are not discussed.

In listening to his recordings in chronological order, one is struck by the consistency of his playing over the years. As early as '37 and '38 his style was an already fully mature one, and while his singing voice changed markedly in the ensuing fifty years, his harmonica remained virtually the same.

Sonny's first recordings (available on Document CD 5230 - highly recommended!) were primarily solo pieces and/or harmonica and washboard duets. They usually featured Terry singing in a falsetto voice (he called it "high-setto,") and accompanying himself with audacious rhythm patterns and beautifully controlled single-line runs. In those early days he also waxed several brilliant instrumental pieces, often imitating the rural sounds he grew up with: trains, hounds, foxes, etc. Because his (falsetto) voice was in virtually the same tonal register as his harp, he sometimes finished off or substituted parts of a vocal line with his harp, or whooped a falsetto singing note during the harp break. On occasion it can be difficult to pinpoint exactly where one stops and the other begins.

As the years went by and Terry began to work more with guitarists, his style changed only to the extent that he no longer found it necessary in every song to provide the driving rhythm. When the song called for it, of course, it was there, and the falsetto whoops remained as well.

Terry used several hand effects, most of which relied upon a single premise: the harp would be held mostly with one hand, while the other formed a cup behind it. Most players find it easiest to hold and support the harp with the left hand, and then use the right to pivot, slap, wah-wah and otherwise alter the tone.

When chording, Sonny puts his tongue to good use. His rhythmic playing features very clipped starts and stops; there's no mushiness to the beginnings or endings of his notes. This is achieved by bouncing the tongue off the roof of the mouth. Try saying out loud the words "dit, dit, dit." Now say them while inhaling. It sounds a little bit like the scolding noise you make ("tsk, tsk") when you're reprimanding your cat for spitting a hairball into your guitar case.

Now do that exact same thing while drawing holes 1, 2, & 3 through your harp. . . that's a Sonny Terry rhythm pattern! We'll expand upon it a little later.

Like most other blues players, Terry often utilized a "call and response" pattern of following the vocal with a similar single-line melodic phrase. The smoothness of these lines is the most notable characteristic of this aspect of his style.

In faster songs, Sonny used the harp as a punctuation of the rhythm, cutting off chords sharply either by tongue clicking or hand smacking. In this next section we'll analyze and break down 70 of his specific licks.

Sonny's inspiration: Deford Bailey

SONNY TERRY LICKS

In front: All of these licks are played on the accompanying CD in the same order as in the text. All (except the last four) are played on an "A" harp in cross position, resulting in the key of E. (While Terry played in every key, the two harps he seemed to prefer the most were A and Bb - probably because they most closely fit his vocal range.)

In order to play along with the CD, then, you'll need a ten-hole harp in the key of A. Sonny preferred the Hohner Marine Band model for most of his career (in later years switching to a Lee Oskar,) but any diatonic harp will do... on the CD I'm using a Special 20. What will become immediately evident is that you'll be drawing (instead of blowing) at least 80% of the time.

The CD was recorded using state-of-the-art equipment, so if it should come out slightly sharp or flat in relation to your A harp, you either have a funky harp or your CD deck needs a tweak on it's variable pitch control (if it has one.)

A few more words on the tablature: obviously much of Sonny's style revolves around the bent note, primarily the draw bends on the lower six holes. As we mentioned in the section on tablature, a downward pointed arrow designates a draw.

For the purposes of this tab, a bent note is designated by a bent arrow, as in 4 (which means draw and bend hole 4.)

Most of the time this bent arrow means that you start the note pre-bent, then release it up to it's normal pitch, but sometimes it will mean to start the note at it's normal pitch, then bend it down. You'll have to rely on your ear for those distinctions. In a few cases, only the bent or flatted part of a note is to be played.

In such a case it will be notated with a "straight/bent" arrow, as in: 4

If you see a notation looking thusly: 6

it means that the player is to blow on holes 3 and 6, but nothing else. This is an octave split, and is made possible by blocking out holes 4 and 5 with the tongue. Try aiming the tip of the tongue for the bottom half of the little post that separates holes 4 and 5. That's usually all it takes to block out 4 and 5. Unless you have an unusually huge (or puny) tongue, once you monkey around with this you'll now find yourself blowing through 3 and 6 only.

Finally, should you see a little arc over some notes (⌒) it means those notes are to be slurred together and played very quickly.

When playing in Sonny's style, you'll notice there is very little redirection of wind. In other words, although you might hear him play a lightning-fast riff of 10 or more notes, in most cases all of those notes are draw. Try to think in terms of taking one long sustained breath rather than a series of shorter ones, then start and stop specific notes by bending and tongue slapping off the roof of the mouth.

OK? Are you ready?
Fire up your CD machine, pop open your beverage of choice, and let's go:

A Dozen Intro Licks

I'll start out with a half-a-dozen licks that Sonny often used at the very beginning of slow blues songs:

1.

2.

3.

4. Here's a variation on #3:

5. This is another variation on #3:

6.

Now comes another half-a-dozen licks that Sonny used as intros on faster songs. Some of these are simply patterns that repeat themselves. It's important to remember on many of these patterns that the tongue bounces off the roof of the mouth, and that's what creates the sharp starts and stops.

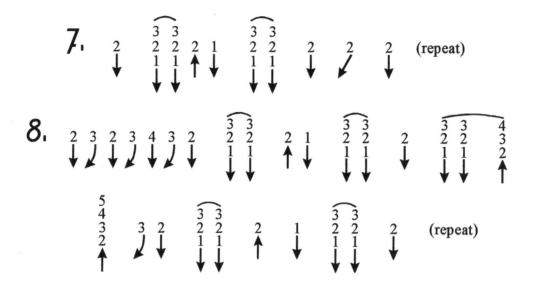

9. This next one is also known as "chugging". In some ways, it's similar to #7.

12. On this one, Sonny utilizes the "E" root note both by drawing hole #2 and by blowing hole #3.

A Dozen Slow And Easy Licks

These will be in two groups of six. The first lick of this group of six is a simple foundation lick that Sonny played often, and following it are several variations of it. These licks would be played over the I chord in a 12-bar progression.

Now, here's six other slow ones:

19.

20.

21.

This employs some tongue blocking (or octave splitting):

22.

23.

Brownie and Sonny, with road crew. England, 1964 Photo by Brian Smith

This will be more than just a lick; it'll be an entire slow blues verse of Sonny licks, starting with #13 and then expanding. It also includes several other of the numbered licks. It's a full 12 bar verse.

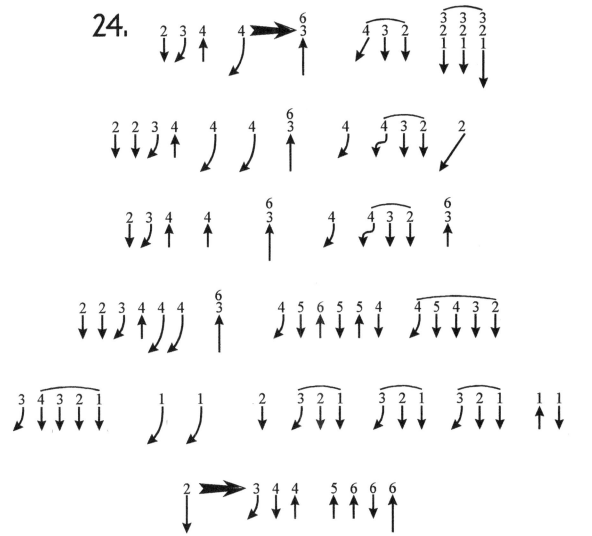

ABC - TV Photo, Courtesy of Brian Smith

Nineteen Fast Licks

25. Actually an expanded version of the lick in #12:

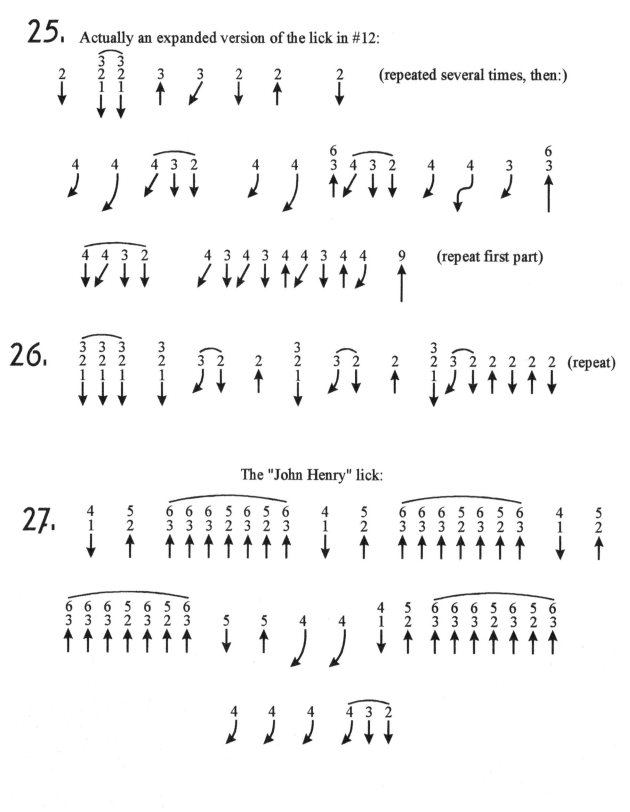

26.

The "John Henry" lick:

27.

These next three licks (28, 29 & 30) employ the bent part **only** of a given note.

28.

29. 3 2 3 2 3 2 3 2 3 3 2 3 3 2 3 2 3 3 2 3 3 3 2 2 (repeat)

30. This is similar to #29, but it has some wind redirection.

3 2 3 2 2 3 2 2 3 2 2 3 3 2 3 2 2 3 2 2 3 2 2 2

31.
$\frac{5}{4}$ $\frac{5}{4}$ $\frac{5}{4}$ $\frac{5}{4}$ 3 2 $\frac{3}{2}\,1$ $\frac{3}{2}\,1$ $\frac{3}{2}\,1$ $\frac{4}{3}\,2$ $\frac{4}{3}\,2$ $\frac{4}{3}\,2$ $\frac{5}{4}$ $\frac{5}{4}$ $\frac{5}{4}$ $\frac{5}{4}$ 3 2 (repeat)

32. This one sounds harder than it really is.

4 5 4 5 4 5 4 3 2 $\frac{3}{2}\,1$ $\frac{3}{2}\,1$ $\frac{3}{2}\,1$ $\frac{4}{3}\,2$ $\frac{4}{3}\,2$ $\frac{4}{3}\,2$ 4 5 4 5 4 5 4 3 2

33. What makes this one interesting is that the root note (or the "tonic") is played on #3 blow rather than on #2 draw (which is where Sonny usually played it). For this lick, at least, that enables the player to go faster.

3 3 3 2 2 3 3 3 2 2 3 3 3 2 2 3 3 3 2 2 3

34.
3   4   4   4 $\frac{6}{3}$ 4 5 6 5 5 4 4 3 2 3 4 (repeat)

35.
2   $\frac{3}{2}\,1$ $\frac{3}{2}\,1$ $\frac{3}{2}\,1$ 3   3   4   4   5   3   2   2 $\frac{3}{2}\,1$ $\frac{3}{2}\,1$ $\frac{3}{2}\,1$ $\frac{3}{2}\,1$ $\frac{3}{2}\,1$ $\frac{3}{2}\,1$ (repeat)

36.
3 3 2 2 $\frac{3}{2}\,1$ 3 3 2 3 $\frac{3}{2}\,1$ 3 3 2 2 $\frac{3}{2}\,1$ 3 3 2 2 2 $\frac{3}{2}\,1$ (repeat)

This employs a tongue-block slide up the face of the harp.

37.

38.

39.

40. This is a lick Sonny played in "Custard Pie."

41.

42. (repeat)

43. This is a percussive kind of attack that Sonny often used. It's important to remember to bounce the tongue off the roof of the mouth for this one.

Ten Shuffle-Paced Licks

44. ³ 2 2 2 3 4 5 4 5   2 3 4 5 5 5 4 2 3   (repeat)
       ²
       ¹
       ↓ ↓ ↓ ↓ ↓ ↓ ↑ ↓ ↑   ↓ ↓ ↓ ↓ ↑ ↓ ↑ ↓ ↓↵

45. Sonny used to play this in live performance, but it's probably better known as the lick Walter Horton played in the song "Easy". It's made up primarily of "trills", that is to say you warble back and forth between two different holes. Also, the "cup" that you form with your hands behind your harmonica is closed.

   3 4 3 4 3 4 etc...   4 5 4 5 4 5 etc...   5 4 5 4 5 4 etc...   (4 5 3 2)
   ↓ ↓ ↓ ↓ ↓ ↓   ↑ ↑ ↑ ↑ ↑ ↑   ↓ ↓ ↓ ↓ ↓ ↓   (↓ ↓ ↓ ↓)

   4 5 4 5 4 5 etc..   5 6 5 6 5 6 etc..   4 5 4 5 4 5 etc..   4 5 4 5 4 5 etc..
   ↓ ↓ ↓ ↓ ↓ ↓   ↑ ↑ ↑ ↑ ↑ ↑   ↓ ↓ ↓ ↓ ↓ ↓   ↑ ↑ ↑ ↑ ↑ ↑

   3 4 3 4 3 4 etc...   (3 2)   5 6 5 6 5 6 etc...   5   5   6 7 6 7 6 7 etc...
   ↓ ↓ ↓ ↓ ↓ ↓ ↓   (↓ ↓)   ↑ ↑ ↑ ↑ ↑ ↑   ↓   ↑   ↑ ↑ ↑ ↑ ↑ ↑

   6 6 5 5   4 5 4 5 4 5 etc...   4 5 5 5 4 4 4   6 5 5 4 5 3 2 2
   3 3 2 2
   ↑ ↑ ↓ ↓   ↓ ↓ ↓ ↓ ↓ ↓ ↓   ↓ ↑ ↓ ↑ ↑ ↑ ↑   ↑ ↓ ↑ ↓ ↑ ↓ ↓ ↓

                    3 4 4 3 3 2 1 1 1
                    ↓ ↑ ↑ ↑ ↓ ↓ ↓ ↓ ↓

The "Boogie" lick:

46.

2 2 3 3 4 4 5 5 5 5 5 5 4 4 3 3   2 2 3 3 4 4 5 5 5 5 5 5 4 4 3 3
↓ ↓ ↓ ↓ ↓ ↓ ↑ ↓ ↓ ↑ ↑ ↓ ↓ ↓ ↓   ↓ ↓ ↓ ↓ ↓ ↓ ↑ ↓ ↓ ↑ ↑ ↓ ↓ ↓ ↓

4 4 5 5 6 6 6 6 7 7 6 6 6 6 5 5   2 2 3 3 4 4 5 5 5 5 5 5 4 4 3 3
↑ ↑ ↑ ↑ ↑ ↑ ↓ ↓ ↑ ↑ ↓ ↓ ↑ ↑ ↑ ↑   ↓ ↓ ↓ ↓ ↓ ↓ ↑ ↓ ↓ ↑ ↑ ↓ ↓ ↓ ↓

1 1 2 2 3 3 3 3 4 4 3 3 3 3 2 2   2 2 3 3 4 4 5 4 3 3 ⁶₃ ⁶₃
↓ ↓ ↙ ↙ ↙ ↙ ↓ ↓ ↑ ↑ ↓ ↙ ↙ ↙ ↙   ↓ ↓ ↓ ↓ ↓ ↓ ↑ ↓ ↑ ↑

Now let's try, as "lick 47", the first part of that boogie lick, only we're going to have backbeats and employ tongue-blocking.

47.

2 ³₂₁ 3 ⁴₃₂ ⁴₁₂ ⁵₂ ⁴₃₂ ⁵₂ ⁴₃₂ ⁵₂ ⁴₃₂ ⁴₁₂ ⁴₃₂ 3 ³₂₁ 2 (repeat)
↓ ↓   ↓ ↓   ↓   ↑ ↓   ↓   ↓ ↑   ↓   ↓   ↓   ↘ ↓   ↓

Willie Dixon, Sonny Terry, Brownie McGhee, Courtesy of Mary Katherine Aldin

This is a full 12-bar verse:

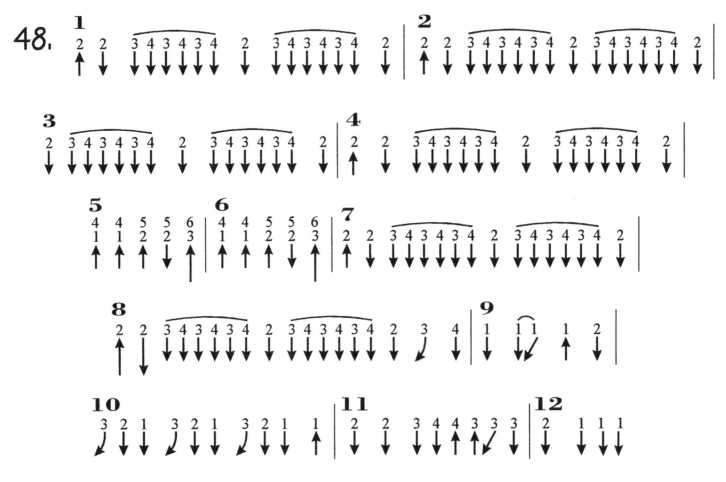

49. This is a complete 8-bar verse. You could use this on "Sittin' On Top Of The World", "Trouble In Mind" or any of the 8-bar blues songs.

A simple chord alternation between the I chord and the IV chord:

50.

2 2 3 2 3 4 4 3 2 2 2 $\overset{4}{\underset{2}{\overset{3}{}}}$ $\overset{4}{\underset{2}{\overset{3}{}}}$ 3 2 3 4

$\overset{3}{\underset{1}{\overset{2}{}}}$ $\overset{3}{\underset{1}{\overset{2}{}}}$ 4 4 4 3 2 2 3 $\overset{4}{\underset{2}{\overset{3}{}}}$ $\overset{4}{\underset{2}{\overset{3}{}}}$

51. A stair-step turnaround:

$\begin{pmatrix}3\\2\\1\end{pmatrix}$ 2 3 2 3 4 3 4 4 3 4 4

52. This is based upon a famous big-band number:

1 2 3 4 5 4 5 2 3 1 2 3 4 5 4 5 2 3

4 3 4 5 6 6 6 6 4 5 1 2 3 4 5 4 5 2 3

53. Fifty-three comes from a song Sonny played called "My Baby's Gone".

2 $\overset{5}{\underset{3}{\overset{4}{}}}$ 3 2 2 2 2 $\overset{5}{\underset{3}{\overset{4}{}}}$ 3 2 2 2 4 4 5 5 $\overset{6}{\underset{3}{}}$

4 4 5 5 $\overset{6}{\underset{3}{}}$ 2 $\overset{5}{\underset{3}{\overset{4}{}}}$ 3 2 2 2 2 $\overset{5}{\underset{3}{\overset{4}{}}}$ 3 2 2 2

Five Backup Licks

In some ways, this heading is an oxymoron - if you're playing backup, how can you be playing a lick? In Sonny's case, backup playing was about as important as playing lead. It's something of an unsung skill, but it's necessary. These days, a lot of beginning harp players seem content to wail their way through a song without regard to their fellow players - that's a good way not to get yourself asked back to the jam. So here's a few ways that Sonny solved the challenge of tasteful backup playing.

You can hear that Sonny often tongue-clicked simple chords:

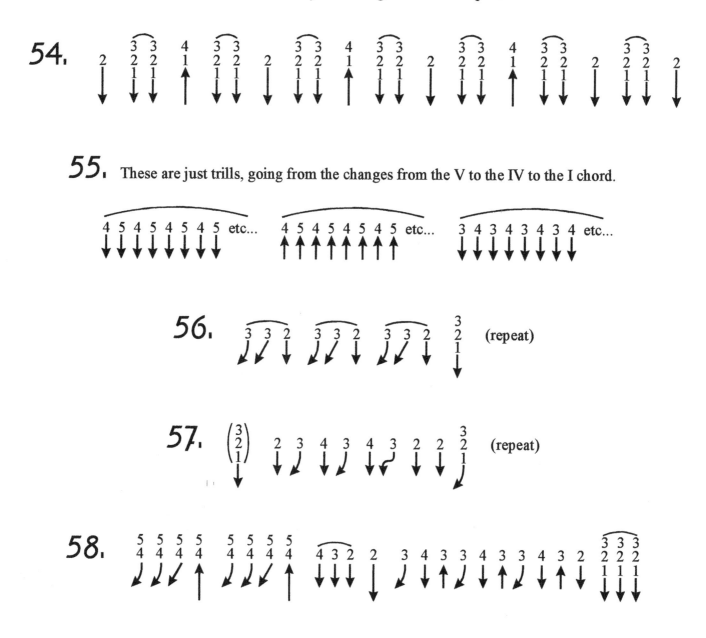

55. These are just trills, going from the changes from the V to the IV to the I chord.

Seven Tricky Licks

This is a little pattern that involves a tongue-block.

59.

60. Here's a tongue trill. It's achieved by bouncing the tongue quickly off the face of the harp.

61. This one is a throat-pop, where you sort of constrict the throat, inhale and pinch and punch at the same time.

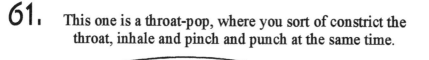

62. This is an ending that Sonny used a lot, and it's a blow-bend on hole #9.

63. This is a "growl", which is usually done on hole #3, but sometimes holes 2 or 4. It's done inhaled, you bend the note and then constrict your throat. For me at least, it first came kind of accidentally, but then you learn how to control it.

Here's a "hand-smack", where you remove your right hand and
then slap it back into the harp while playing an inhaled chord.

64.
6	6	6	3	2	3	4	6	6	6	3	2	2 2 1	(repeat)
5	5	5					5	5	5				
4	4	4					4	4	4				

65. This is a fast thing that Sonny sometimes did, involving a bit of wind redirection:

2 2 3 4 4   6 6 6 6 5 4 4 5 4 3 2 3 2 2 2 1 1 1
                   3

3 4 4   6   6 6 6 5 4 4 5 4 3 2 3 2   3
             3   2
                                                 1

Sonny & Brownie, October 1962
ABC - TV Photo, Courtesy of Brian Smith

Lick 66 will be more than just a lick - it'll be the entire solo from the song "All Talk And No Action." The whole song follows here and on the CD.

By Tom Ball & Kenny Sultan - © Good Time Blues Music, BMI - From "Filthy Rich," - Flying Fish 619 - Used by permission

For those of you who want the words, they are:

Well, you been flappin' your trap, ever since you were little,
You must have been vaccinated with a phonograph needle,
You're all talk and no action, everywhere in the world you go,
Well, you got a head like a brick, a mouth like a radio.

Well, you might stop talkin' on the day that you choke,
If silence is golden then you must be broke.
You're all talk and no action, everywhere in the world you go,
Well, you got a head like a brick, a mouth like a radio.

(Guitar Solo)

Yeah, I'm gonna get me some plugs, and stick 'em in my ears,
You sound like a convention of tobacco auctioneers,
You're all talk and no action, everywhere in this world you go,
Well, you got a head like a brick, a mouth like a radio.

(Harmonica solo)

Yeah, I know they say that money talks, and I know it ain't no lie,
'Cause every time I get some it tells me good-bye,
It's all talk and no action, yes, everywhere in the world I go,
Well, you got a head like a brick, a mouth like a radio.

Yes, if you don't stop blabbin', lord, down the road I go.

All Talk And No Action

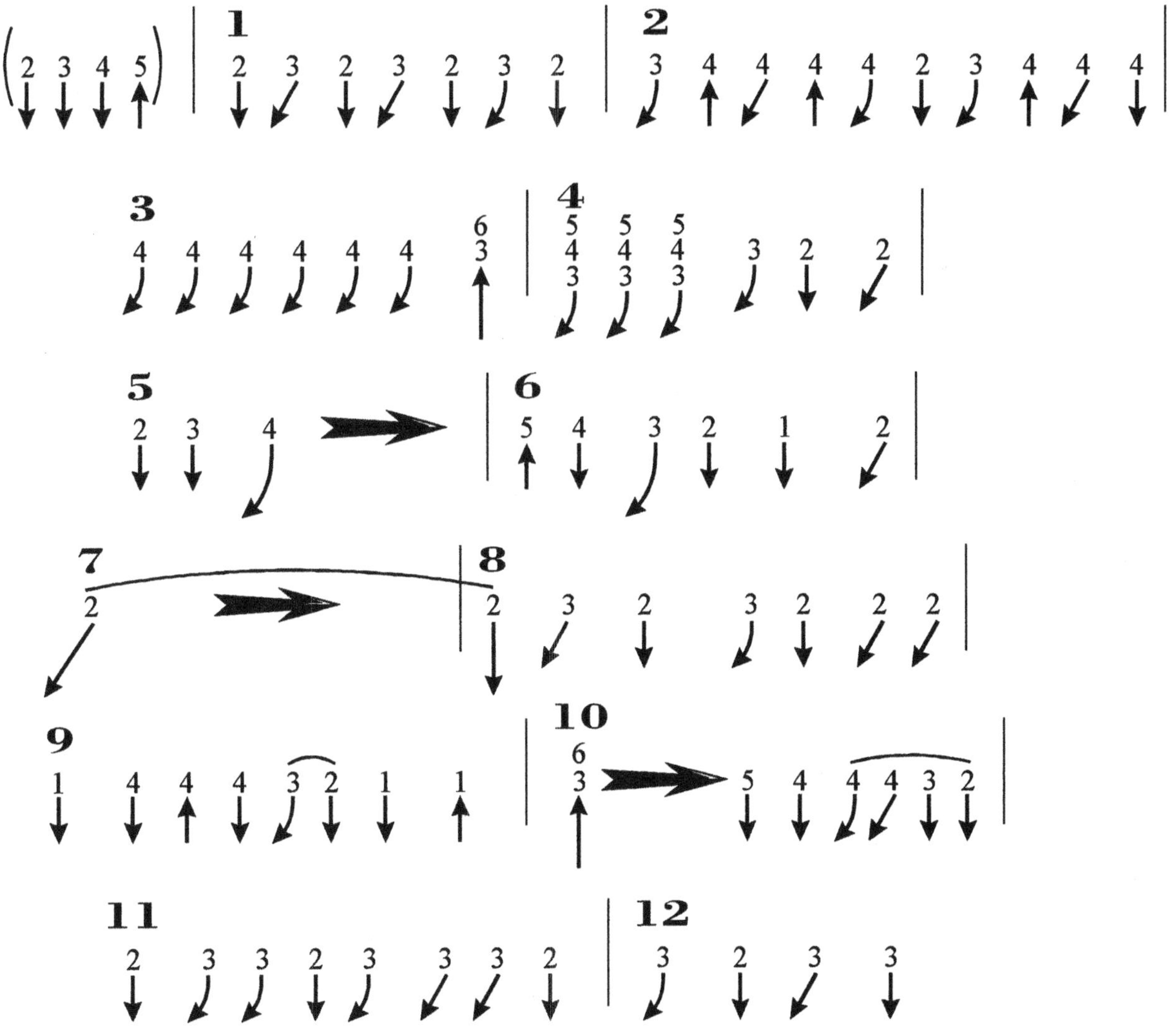

These four licks are actually four-plus complete verses lifted out of my recording with guitarist Kenny Sultan of a traditional song long associated with Sonny, "Tater Pie" (also from our Flying Fish release "Filthy Rich.")

Again these are not note-for-note Sonny Terry, but they are played in a similar style. Incidentally, these four are among the only licks on this CD not played with an A harp - Here I'm primarily using a Bb, playing in the key of F.

Now, what I've done here is splice together the intro from the song, and the harp-break section, eliminating the vocals. For the purposes of this book, lick 67 will refer to the first 20 bars - in other words the beginning 12 bars (which are harp only) plus the 8 bars following it. At that point you'll hear a rather awkward splice, and after that the song becomes a standard 12-bar blues, with 3 instrumental verses in a row. For transcription purposes, these three 12-bar verses will be considered licks 68, 69 and 70.

Please keep in mind that lick 69. or the second-to-the-last verse, is played on a different harp than the rest of the verses. You can probably hear the difference - it's a lot higher. That's because on that verse only, I switched to a Low-F harp (which is tuned exactly an octave lower than a normal F harp) and played the verse in first-position.

Incidentally, the rhythm section on this recording (as well as on "All Talk And No Action,") is our pals Tom Lee on upright bass, and Jody Eulitz beating out the rhythm on a cardboard Jack Daniels box.

Tater Pie - 1st 20 bars (lick 67) (B♭ harp)

Solo harp: 1st 12 bars

40

Tater Pie (continued)

1st regular 12-bar verse: (B♭ harp)

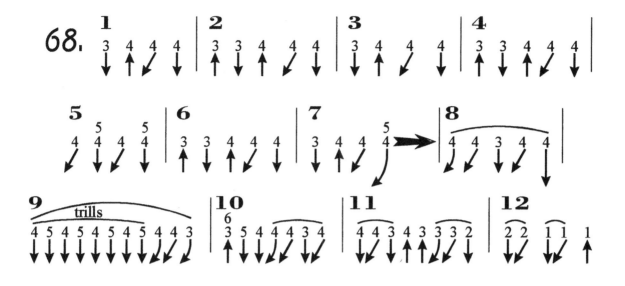

2nd regular 12-bar verse (played on a Low - F harp)

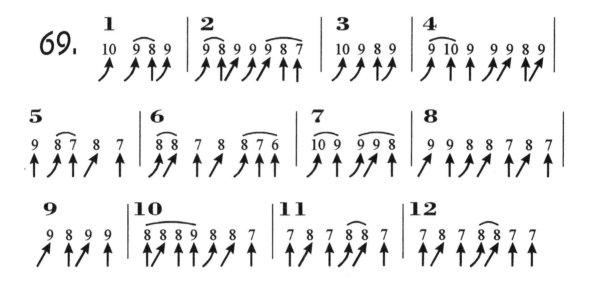

3rd regular 12-bar verse (back to a B♭ harp)

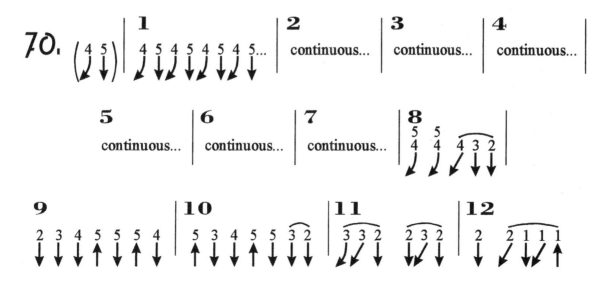

Greetings Distribs, Music Merchants and Deejays!

Sonny Terry & Brownie McGhee

"CLIMBING ON TOP OF THE HILL"

1023

Old Town Records

701 - 7th Ave. (CO 5-8810) N. Y.

Courtesy Galen Gart's "First Pressings"

David Gahr - Photo

RCA VICTOR

RECORD PREVUE

DISC JOCKEY SAMPLE

NOT FOR SALE

RADIO CORPORATION OF AMERICA

Barnhill Music BMI

E3-VB-1908 (20-5577)

SONNY IS DRINKING

(Sonny Terry-Leroy Kirkland)

SONNY TERRY

Time: 2:30

FAIRFIELD HALL, CROYDON

General Manager: T. J. Pyper, M.I.M.E.N.

MONDAY 19th OCTOBER

at 6.45 p.m. and 9.00 p.m.

"A DOCUMENTARY OF THE AUTHENTIC BLUES"

THE NATIONAL JAZZ FEDERATION

in association with HORST LIPPMANN presents the THIRD

AMERICAN NEGRO BLUES FESTIVAL

LIGHTNING HOPKINS	★	HOWLING WOLF
SLEEPY JOHN ESTES	★	HUBERT SUMLIN
JOHN HENRY BARBEE	★	HAMMIE NIXON
SUGAR PIE DESANTO	★	CLIFTON JAMES
SUNNYLAND SLIM	★	WILLIE DIXON
SONNY BOY WILLIAMSON		

TICKETS : 6/- 8/- 10/6 12/6 15/- 17/6 21/-

SONNY TERRY · HARMONICA & VOCAL SOLOS

ALCOHOLIC BLUES · WOMEN'S BLUES (CORRINA) · LOST JOHN
LOCOMOTIVE BLUE · BAD LUCK BLUES · HARMONICA STOMP
SHORTNIN' BREAD · FINE & FALSE VOICE · BEAUTIFUL CITY
FOLKWAYS RECORDS & SERVICE CORP., N. Y.   FA2035

FREDERIC RAMSEY, JR.

Sonny's first L.P. 1952

Moving on GROOVE

New Hit

BIG CONNIE singing

MUMBLES BLUES

b/w

WAIT 'TIL NEXT WEEK, BABY

G/4G-0143

Hot

THE NITE CAPS

BE MY GIRL

G/4G-0136

PIANO RED

SHE KNOCKS ME OUT

G/4G-0136

Just Released

THE AVALONS

CHAIN AROUND MY HEART

b/w

OOH! SHE FLEW

G/4G-0141

SONNY TERRY

HOOTIN' BLUES #2

b/w

RIDE AND ROLL

G/4G-0138

ARTHUR (Big Boy) CRUDUP

MEAN OLD FRISCO BLUES

b/w

ROCK ME MAMA

G/4G-5004

GROOVE

A PRODUCT OF RADIO CORPORATION OF AMERICA

155 East 24th Street, N. Y. 10, N. Y.

Courtesy Galen Gart's "First Pressings"

-BONUS TRACK-
SALTY HOLMES'
"TALKING" HARMONICA

The tenth track on the CD is a bonus track which features some pretty startling harp, taken from an old 78 by the obscure Salty Holmes. It has nothing whatsoever to do with Sonny Terry, but it's so damn entertaining I wanted to include it anyway!

The closest Sonny ever came to playing something like this was on his "Mama Blues," during which he made his harp speak a few rudimentary words. Holmes' talking harmonica, however, is unquestionably the most articulate example of this effect.

So how does he do it? I don't have the slightest idea except to say he is playing cross on a Bb harp and somehow managing to formulate words while inhaling, mostly on hole #3. Give it a try and if you have any success, drop me a line and let me know how to do it, O.K.?

As I mentioned, this is taken from an ancient 78 I found in a junk shop in Winnemucca, Nevada, so please don't expect too much in terms of sound quality...it's the music that counts!

> The legendary Jerry Byrd is playing the steel guitar, I contacted Jerry and he said he doesn't remember much about the session, since he was doing so many at that time. It was recorded in Cincinnati, Ohio. Jerry said Louie Innis is playing rhythm guitar and Zako Turner electric guitar. Ed note.

- BONUS TRACK #2 -
AMPLIFIED INSTRUMENTAL

Players whose interests lean more towards the Chicago style of amplified harp will hopefully enjoy this final bonus track. The harp used is an Ab Special 20 blown into an Astatic JT-30 mic, and played through a '62 Fender outboard reverb tank and a '56 tweed Fender Deluxe amp. Kenny's guitar is a '46 Gibson ES-300. Although we usually play acoustic, every now and then we have to blow off some steam and raise hell in the neighborhood by plugging in! This is not included in tab, but listen closely and you'll hear many of the licks taught in this book.

As always, please feel free to write me with any questions or comments regarding this book, and yes I am still seeking to complete my collection of Sonny Terry (and Walter Horton) 78s; if you have any for sale or trade please let me know. I hope to see you in your town soon - thanks, best wishes and happy harpin'!

Tom Ball
P.O. Box 20156
Santa Barbara, CA 93120   USA

Selected Discography and Key Chart

During the course of his life, Sonny Terry recorded (either as a sideman or a leader) nearly 700 titles on harmonica. In addition to his work with Blind Boy Fuller and/or Brownie McGhee, he also accompanied many others including Buddy Moss, Leadbelly, Champion Jack Dupree, Sticks McGhee, Allen Bunn, Bob Gaddy, Ralph Willis, Square Walton, John Sellers, Billy Bland, Alonzo Scales, Rev.Gary Davis, Big Bill Broonzy, Lightnin' Hopkins, Johnny Winter, Long Gone Miles, and many others. A comprehensive discography would run nearly the length of this book!

What follows is a limited discography and key chart for over 200 songs on 16 of the most commonly found LPs and/or CDs in rough chronological order. It is recommended that the harp student acquire at least a few of these and play along with them. In all cases, the key (both of the song and of the harp) is listed.

note: (1) = straight harp (first position) (2) = mismastered (flat to pitch.)

CD's:

Sonny Terry 1938-1945. Document DOCD-5230	Song Key	Harp Key
Mountain Blues	F	Bb
The New John Henry	F	Bb
Fox Chase	F	Bb
Lost John	F	Bb
Train Whistle Blues	Bb(1)	Bb(1)
New Love Blues	F	Bb
Harmonica Blues	Eb	Ab
Harmonica And Washboard Breakdown	Eb	Ab
Harmonica Stomp	E	A
Harmonica And Washboard Blues	E	A
Forty-Four Whistle Blues	E(2)	A(2)
Blowing the Blues	E(2)	A(2)
Touch It Up and Go	E	A
John Henry	E	A
Fox Chase (6503-A-2)	E	A
Fox Chase (6503-A-3)	E	A
The Red Cross Store	E	A
Glory	Eb	Ab
Lonesome Train	D	G
Run Away Women	D(2)	G(2)
Shake Down	E(2)	A(2)
Sweet Woman	E	A
Fox Chase (SO-8)	F	Bb
Hard Luck Child	F(2)	Bb(2)
We Just Can't Agree	E	A
My Baby Likes to Shuffle	E	A

Sonny Terry The Folkways Years-1944-1963. Smithsonian Folkways 40033		
Old Jabo	E	A
Going Down Slow	E	A
Crow Jane Blues	E	A
Harmonica With Slaps	E	A
Pick A Bale of Cotton	F	Bb
Dark Road	E	A
Skip To My Lou	E	A
The Woman is Killin' Me	E	A
Jail House Blues	F	Bb
Fox Chase/Right on that Shore	E	A
Shortnin' Bread	E	(jaw harp)
Sweet Woman	E	A
Lost John	E	A
A Man Is Nothing But A Fool	F	Bb
Poor Man (But A Good Man)	E	A
I've Been Your Doggie Since I've Been Your Man	F	Bb

Sonny Terry & Brownie McGhee - California Blues - Fantasy 24723-2

I Got Fooled	E	A
No Need of Running	E	A
I Feel So Good	F	Bb
Thinkin' and Worrying	F	Bb
I Love You Baby	F	Bb
California Blues	F	Bb
Walkin' and Lyin' Down	B	E
First and Last Love	F	Bb
Christine	F	Bb
I Have Had My Fun	F	Bb
Whoppin' and Squallin'	E	A
Water Boy Cry	E	(no harp)
Motherless Child	F	Bb
Sportin' Life	E	A
John Henry	E	A
I'm a Stranger	E	A
Cornbread and Peas	E	A
Louise	F	Bb
I Done Done	E	A
Meet You in the Morning	F	Bb
Poor Boy From Home	E	A
Hudy Leadbelly	F	Bb
Something's Wrong At Home	E	A
Take This Hammer	F	Bb
Baby's Gone	E	A
Lose Your Money	F	Bb

Lightnin' Hopkins - Last Night Blues - Prestige BV 1029

Rocky Mountain	E	A
Got to Move Your Baby	E	A
So Sorry to Leave You	E	A
Take A Trip With Me	E	A
Last Night Blues	E	A
Lightnin's Stroke	A	D
Hard to Love a Woman	E	A
Conversation Blues	E	A

LP's
Sonny Terry - Whoopin' The Blues - Charly CRB 1120

Whoopin' the Blues	E	A
All Alone Blues	E	A
Worried Man Blues	F	Bb
Leavin' Blues	E	A
Screaming And Crying Blues	E	A
Riff and Harmonica Jump	E	A
Crow Jane Blues	F	Bb
Beer Garden Blues	F	Bb
Hot Headed Woman	F	Bb
Custard Pie Blues	F	Bb
Early Morning Blues	F	Bb
Harmonica Rag	E	A
Dirty Mistreater	F	Bb
Telephone Blues	E	A

Sonny Terry - Harmonica and Vocal Solos - Folkways FA 2035

Alcoholic Blues	E	A
Women's Blues (Corrina)	F	Bb
Locomotive Blues	A(1)	A(1)
Bad Luck Blues	E	A
Lost John	E	A
Shortnin' Bread	A(1)	A(1)
Fine and False Voice	E	A
Harmonica Stomp	E	A
Beautiful City	E	A

B. McGhee & S. Terry - Back Country Blues - Savoy MG 14019

Gone, Baby, Gone	F	Bb
Tell Me Baby	A	D
Sittin' Pretty	F	Bb
Bottom Blues	F	Bb
Dissatisfied Blues	E	(no harp)
Diamond Ring	E	(no harp)
The Way I Feel	B	(no harp)
So Much Trouble	E	(no harp)
When It's Love Time	G	C
I'd Love To Love You	F	Bb
Love's A Disease	F	Bb
My Fault	F	Bb

B McGhee & S. Terry - Guitar Highway - Verve FVS 9019

Better Day	E	A
Confusion	D	G
Dark Road	E	A
John Henry	E	A
Let Me Make A Little Money	E	A
Old Jabo	E	A
I Love You Baby	E	A
Guitar Highway	E	A
Heart In Sorrow	A	D
Preachin' The Blues	E	A
Can't Help Myself	C	F
Best of Friends	F	Bb
If You Lose Your Money	E	A

S. Terry & B. McGhee - Folk Song of - Roulette 25074

I Love You Baby	F(2)	Bb(2)
Cornbread, Peas, Black Molasses	F(2)	Bb(2)
That's How I Feel	A	(no harp)
You'd Better Mind	F	Bb
Treated Wrong	E(2)	A(2)
Brownie's Blues	B	E
Southern Train	E	A
Just A Dream	F	Bb
Sonny's Blues	F	Bb
Gone But Not Forgotten	D	(no harp)
Change The Lock On The Door	E	A
Climbing On Top Of The Hill	F(2)	Bb(2)

Sonny Terry - Sonny's Story - Prestige Bluesville 1025

I Ain't Gonna Be Your Dog No More	E	A
My Baby Done Gone	E	A
Worried Blues	E	A
High Powered Woman	E	A
Pepperheaded Woman	E	A
Sonny's Story	A	D
Gonna Get On My Feets After Awhile	E	A
Four O'Clock Blues	E	A
Telephone Blues	E	A
Great Tall Engine	E	A

S. Terry & B McGhee - Blues Is A Story - World Pacific 1294

Key To The Highway	E	A
Lose Your Money	E	A
Louise	F	Bb
Sportin' Life	F	Bb
New Harmonica Breakdown	F	Bb
Prison Bound	E	A
Livin' With The Blues	F	Bb
Blowin' the Blues	E	A
Baby Please Don't Go	F	Bb
Twelve Gates To The City	F	Bb
Pawnshop Blues	A	D
Brownie's Guitar Blues	E	A

Sonny Terry - Sonny is King - Prestige Bluesville 1059

One Monkey Don't Stop The Show	E	A
Changed The Lock on My Door	E	A
Tater Pie	E	A
She's So Sweet	E	A
Diggin' My Potatoes	E	A
Sonny's Coming	F	Bb
Ida Mae	F	Bb
Callin' My Mama	E	A
Bad Luck	F	Bb
Blues From the Bottom	E	A

Lightnin' Hopkins et al - First Meetin' - World Pacific 1817

Ain't Nothin' Like Whisky	A	D
Penetentiary Blues	A	D
If You Steal My Chickens	A	D
First Meetin'	E	(no harp)
How Long Have It Been Since You Been Home?	Eb	(no harp)
Wimmin From Coast to Coast	A	D

B McGhee & S. Terry - The Best of - Prestige 7715

I Got A Woman	E	A
Backwater Blues	B	E
East Coast Blues	C	F
Don't You Lie To Me	E	A
Jump Little Children	E	A
Blues All Around My Head	F	Bb
Little Black Engine	D	G
Muddy Water	A	D

S. Terry & B McGhee - At Sugar Hill - Fantasy 3340

Hooray, Hooray, This Woman is Killin' Me	E	A
Born To Live The Blues	E	A
Just About Crazy	F	Bb
Up, Sometimes Down	D	G
Baby I Knocked On Your Door	E	A
Keep On Walkin'	E	A
Baby, I Got My Eyes On you	E	A
I Got A little Girl	F	Bb
I Feel Alright Now	B	E
Worry, Worry, Worry	D	G
Sweet Woman Blues	F	Bb

Brownie McGhee - Brownie's Blues - Prestige Bluesville 1042

Jump, Little Children	E	A
Lonesome Day	A	D
One Thing For Sure	E	A
The Killin' Floor	A	D
Little Black Engine	D	G
I Don't Know The Reason	D	G
Trouble In Mind	D	G
Everyday I Have The Blues	E	A
Door To Success	E	A

BIBLIOGRAPHY

Ball, Tom. **Blues Harmonica.** Fullerton: Centerstream, 1993

Bastin, Bruce. **Red River Blues.** Urbana & Chicago: U. of Illinois, 1986

Cooper, Kent & Palmer, Fred. **The Harp Styles of Sonny Terry.** New York: Oak, 1975

Dixon, R.M.W. & Godrich, John. **Blues And Gospel Records, 1902-1942.** London: Storyville. Revised edition, 1969.

Elmes, Barry. **Interview With Sonny Terry.** Living Blues Magazine, 1973.

Field, Kim. **Harmonicas, Harps, and Heavy Breathers.** New York: Fireside, 1993

Glover, Tony. **Blues Harp.** New York: Oak, 1965.

Guthrie, Woody. **Pastures Of Plenty.** New York: Harper, 1990.

Leadbitter, Mike & Slaven, Neil. **Blues Records 1943-1966.** New York: Oak, 1968.

Russell, Tony. **Blacks, Whites and Blues.** London: Studio Vista, 1970.

OTHER HARMONICA BOOKS FROM